At what ~~...~~ *proach of danger?* ~~...~~ *'antic military giant, to step the Ocean, and crush us at a blow? Never! All the armies of Europe, Asia and Africa ... could not by force, take a drink from the Ohio, or make a track on the Blue Ridge, in a trial of a thousand years.... If destruction be our lot, we must ourselves be its author and finisher. As a nation of freemen, we must live through all time, or die by suicide.*

ABRAHAM LINCOLN
The Lyceum Address, 1838

DURING THE WINTER OF 2019–2020, the People's Republic of China, led by the Chinese Communist Party, began what appeared to be an exercise in bio-warfare against the United States and the rest of the world. It did so as it was negotiating a trade deal with President Donald Trump, who had set himself the task of ending China's theft of intellectual property, forced technology transfers, and unfair trade practices. China's

[1]

fifty-year experiment in establishing itself as the preeminent power on earth was in jeopardy of being undermined by President Trump's anti-globalist agenda.

President Trump stated in early May 2020 that the Wuhan virus was worse than Pearl Harbor and September 11. Both of those surprise attacks were designed to demoralize us as a nation. Neither was successful. Both led to war. The president, with access to the very best intelligence, did not make this comparison lightly.

The effects of the Wuhan virus and its damage to the United States's booming economy, as well as its tragic political and social impact on the American people – who have been quarantined beyond any measure of common sense – is a story that is still being played out as this is being written. That the Chinese believed they could pull off this attack unscathed suggests either a gross strategic error, or a certain confidence that the United States had grown so corrupt that, even under an "America first" president like Donald

Trump, they could get away with it. This essay is a way of understanding China, how we have gotten into this mess, and what will be required to set it right.

*　*　*

China is a great nation with global interests and long-term strategic goals. It has a population of almost 1.5 billion people who are hard-working, inventive, and determined, and have made great sacrifices to get where they have in the world today. They are run by the Chinese Communist Party (CCP), which has ninety million members and millions more supporters that form a committed and coherent ruling elite. They are deeply invested in the success of the communist experiment and creating a "socialist society with Chinese characteristics." Over the past seventy years, China has killed more than one hundred million of its own people at the altar of this experiment to create the country that it is today. This is to say, China is not to be underestimated.

China will not use bombs or bullets. It will compromise our leaders and corrupt our elites in the most peaceful, orderly way possible.

China's goals are to preserve the geographic integrity of the People's Republic of China (P.R.C.), propagate communist ideology among its population, and maintain the military, intelligence gathering, and strategic forces capable of pacifying its domestic population, deterring Asian competitors, and projecting strategic capabilities anywhere necessary.

President Xi Jinping and the CCP see themselves as the rightful rulers of the world. They believe their communist ideology superior to the democratic capitalism of the West. They regard the United States as a technologically advanced and wealthy country that stands in the way of their strategic designs. Not only is the United States capable of waging war against the P.R.C. as no other nation (save Russia) can, it has demonstrated a commitment to defending the principles of human freedom both for itself and for its allies.

As such, the P.R.C. cannot be indifferent to the United States's political and economic development. It would prefer a United States that is deeply divided internally and discredited in its use of diplomacy and military force abroad. It wants to manage America's decline as a world power if it can achieve it. As a practical matter, this will require convincing the U.S. that the P.R.C. cannot be challenged militarily; that America's prosperity is contingent upon Chinese economic interdependence; and that the safest course of action is an accommodation with the P.R.C. and the bloc of countries that have subscribed to its Belt and Road Initiative. This has been the P.R.C.'s political and strategic campaign for the past decade. It is consistent with the

P.R.C.'s broader political objective – that China's rise is inevitable – that it has been advancing for the past half century.

At the heart of China's political warfare is the goal of demoralizing the United States to the point where America believes that further resistance is futile. This seems not so much a grand strategic insight as much as common sense. Corrupting an enemy is as old as time immemorial. One does not need to have read Sun Tzu or Herodotus to understand that there are men who can be compromised. Quite often, such corruption brings down a country from within and war does not even need to be waged. Far from being a despicable act, corrupting one's enemy may actually prevent open hostilities and the loss of life that accompanies real war and the battles that must be fought. What is despicable is the nation that lets itself be corrupted. That will cause a nation to fall today as surely as it led cities to fall in the ancient world. It is in this light that we must see what Communist

China is attempting right now in the United States.

Lest anyone doubt what is going on, we are in a war today with the People's Republic of China and its masters in the Chinese Communist Party. Their goal is not to use bombs or bullets if they can be avoided. They would much rather compromise our leaders and corrupt our elites and have their way with us in the most peaceful and orderly way possible. They do not need to fight us on a battlefield if we are so otherwise demoralized and compliant that war will never even be fought.

This is worth noting, for they have engaged in this current political and information war against the United States confident that America has grown corrupt, and that its political, financial, and cultural elites are in near complete sympathy with the globalist project of an interdependent world, with the P.R.C. at its head. This confidence has arisen from a half century of political deception, manipulation, and penetration of American society.

At the heart of China's statecraft has been a persistent effort to integrate its economy with that of the United States. It has done this through engaging in trade, structuring relationships where U.S. manufacturing could be transferred to China, and integrating the interests of America's business, political, and financial elites with those of the P.R.C. These efforts complemented the economic forces that were already in play by the time the U.S. recognized the P.R.C. in 1979. It was by then that, because of environmental and other regulatory costs in the United States, domestic manufacturing had become prohibitively expensive.

In his book, *The Hundred-Year Marathon*, China scholar Michael Pillsbury convincingly laid out the P.R.C.'s political and diplomatic initiatives that enabled these developments. In the 1970s, U.S. policymakers were led to believe that, through "constructive engagement," China could be fashioned into a democratic ally capable of balancing the Soviet Union's military and ideological threat. The so-called "China card" did not seem unreasonable at the time, especially as the P.R.C.'s economic modernization held out the possibility of advantageous relationships for U.S. businesses with its market of more than one billion people.

But, given the population's relatively impoverished state, this would require sharing ever-advanced technology and allowing large sectors of U.S. manufacturing to face low-cost Chinese competition with little hope for success. Although this would lead to cheaper consumer goods for Americans, it also meant the U.S. economy would shift away from manufacturing, and the middle-class jobs it created, to an economy largely made up of higher-wage information or knowledge-based jobs, and lower-wage service and consumer-based employment.

Since these initiatives arose during the Cold War, the U.S. government and Congress were required to make exceptions to China's ongoing human rights abuses and violations of various trade rules. From the very beginning of U.S.-P.R.C. relations, malfeasance was an acceptable feature of Chinese economic behavior and statecraft. The P.R.C. was eventually allowed into the World Trade Organization (albeit not without some opposition) and China became ever wealthier, its country more modern, and its technological base – much of it stolen from America and the West – ever more advanced. This is not to say that the Chinese are not intelligent and capable of developing such technology themselves. But why should they spend time and resources when they can steal the technology or compel companies doing business in China to simply hand over the technology? Additionally, as Michael Pillsbury points out, it has been U.S. policy to give key scientific discoveries to China as part of bilateral agreements made in the 1980s.

America's political and financial elites accepted both China's abuses and the transfers of technology because they had been sold on the notion that a strong, modernizing China was good for America's prosperity and security. That, over time, this would lead to an open and free China which respected the rights of man. That to push in the opposite direction – as in, reciprocal trade relations and an end to the theft of intellectual property – would lead to retrenchment, greater

---

President Trump stated the Wuhan virus was worse than Pearl Harbor and September 11. He did not make this comparison lightly.

---

repression, and a failure of the globalist promise of ever modernizing and prosperous nations developing in cooperation with one another.

To be sure, American businesses were more

than happy to watch American manufacturing leave if it meant lower-cost products that could be sold for higher profit margins. The near tragic loss of pharmaceutical manufacturing in the United States is a testament to this. No matter how much consumers enjoy lower costs for so many goods, could anyone believe it was wise to export the making of the active pharmaceutical ingredients from whence we get our medicines? Most Americans would be incredulous to learn that we have allowed a strategic industry like manufacturing medicines to have its production be concentrated in Communist China.

To this very day, the P.R.C. is designated a "developing nation" and enjoys certain privileges because of this at the World Trade Organization and various other international forums. For their part, Chinese leaders, from Mao Zedong and Deng Xiaoping to Xi Jinping, have been masters at shaping the narrative that China is still developing and thus requires assistance in order to someday take its rightful place as a global superpower.

They have combined this with notions of staying calm and biding their time while they maintain a low profile. It is all rather comforting for the West to hear that China is continually developing and its true desire is a peaceful rise as world leader.

This stands in contrast to the more radical writings of various sectors of the Chinese Communist Party and the People's Liberation Army, which is openly against American supremacy. In *Unrestricted Warfare*, a book written in 1999 by Qiao Liang and Wang Xiangsui, the authors discuss strategies such as using a combination of traditional military means, along with cyber warfare, economic warfare, biochemical warfare, atomic warfare, and terrorism.

When you combine this thinking with the fact that the Chinese have more than two million men under arms and that their navy, army, and air force are becoming as sophisticated as those of the United States, there is a very real sense in which the P.R.C. must be taken as a peer competitor of the U.S. In addition, China possesses an advanced arsenal of long-range, intercontinental ballistic missiles (most of which are aimed at the United States) and hundreds of short- and medium-range nuclear missiles and cruise missiles for use in an Asian theatre of combat, primarily directed against America's military presence there, as well as Japan and Taiwan. Likewise, it is investing substantial resources to develop a space-based military capability. It is building various launch vehicles, including manned spaceflight, a space station, and extensive antisatellite weaponry meant to negate the United States's own capabilities.

The P.R.C.'s intelligence capabilities are equally impressive. Through the Communist Party, it has built a system that includes the Ministry of State Security, the Ministry of Public Security, and the National Security Commission of the Communist Party of China. Together, they are able to maintain internal security through a secret police agency, operate a system of social credit scoring to monitor the online behavior of millions

China's political warfare goal is to demoralize the United States to the point where America believes that further resistance is futile.

of Chinese, suppress internal dissent the old-fashioned way through the intimidation, arrest, imprisonment, and murder or "disappearing" of dissidents. In addition, they are now mastering the mass confinement of more than one million Uighur Muslims in internment camps that have officially been described as "vocational schools."

Externally, the Ministry of State Security operates foreign intelligence operations that target other nations. Key targets are the U.S. military and the armed forces of allied nations. The U.S.-China Economic and Security Review Commission has described how numerous retired U.S. military officials have transitioned to the private sector and have been compromised by Chinese intelligence. These include retired U.S. Army Lieutenant Colonel Benjamin Bishop, who pleaded guilty to transferring classified materials to a Chinese agent concerning joint U.S.-South Korean military exercises; and Gregg Bergersen, a former analyst at the Department of Defense, who pleaded guilty to passing on materials to a Chinese agent regarding arms sales to Taiwan. These instances are not remarkable in the sense that one would expect a hostile nation to seek military and diplomatic intelligence regarding its foe.

Also expected are China's efforts to acquire sensitive U.S. military technology. Here, China has been particularly aggressive in using both Chinese nationals (operating as legitimate businessmen) to steal technology, and Chinese immigrants who have become naturalized U.S. citizens to acquire advanced weaponry. In 2016, there was the notable case of Wenxia Man, a Chinese-born American citizen living in San Diego who was convicted and sentenced to four years in prison for seeking to buy an MQ-9 Reaper/Predator B unmanned aerial vehicle and other sensitive components for transfer to the P.R.C. Again, that the P.R.C. would want to acquire such technology is to be expected. Over time, however, even with extensive counterintelligence and counterespionage activities going on, there is a sense in which China's efforts seem almost overwhelming. What they cannot obtain from cyberespionage they seek from direct acquisition. What they cannot buy, they bribe their way into obtaining.

China has proven more than proficient in acquiring key trade secrets, personal information that might be useful for blackmail and intimidation, as well as relevant political information for trade negotiations, international disputes, or normal bilateral relations. There is also the complexity that arises with so many Chinese-Americans working for the government or in the American defense industry. Since so many have family back in China, and because Chinese intelligence agencies are so ruthless, these employees are more susceptible to coercion, bribery, and the like. But to investigate large numbers of Chinese-Americans for suspected treasonous acts, even when it is warranted, is to call into question the loyalty of all Chinese-Americans to the United States as a whole. In an open society like the United States, this puts unusual stress on the counterintelligence system.

Given all this, at the heart of the Chinese enterprise is the simple strategy of establishing in the American mind the belief that China is simply too populous, too militarily capable, too wealthy, too proficient at operating an intelligence service capable of reaching anywhere into American society, and too determined as a nation to turn back now. The inevitable rise of China has turned into the inevitable conquest of the world by the P.R.C.

China's immediate goal is to cement in the minds of American presidents and policy-makers that the United States is not the world's sole superpower, that the P.R.C.'s needs and desires must somehow be accommodated, and that we ought not do anything to provoke the P.R.C. lest we undermine the globalist world order that has brought so much prosperity to so many people. In this sense, it is meant to intimidate the global elites that are so heavily invested in this world order. To this way of thinking, globalism – under assault in America for the first time ever – must be defended not merely for the sake of economic prosperity, but also for the sake of peace and stability.

It is worth noting that globalism is a way of understanding economic and political relations between nations where the interests of the global world order are put before the national interests of any given nation. To defend nationalism, or to put "America first" as President Trump has done in his commonsense way, is therefore to be at odds with globalism. This is seen not merely as selfish but counterproductive, since American prosperity must be tied to the success of the global world order. Unfortunately, this globalist view is still very prevalent among most of the policy personnel at the Departments of State, Treasury, and Defense, even during the Trump administration.

For now, that global world order requires that all efforts be focused on the development of the People's Republic of China, for if the most populous country on earth modernizes, it will be able to help the rest of the world develop, too. In the meantime, any transgression committed by the P.R.C. against accepted standards of international law, trade, and finance are to be overlooked. This includes unfair trade deals, theft of intellectual property, or forced technology transfers. It matters not that the P.R.C. is becoming wealthy and has built world-class capabilities in a wide array of businesses and industries. It is a developing nation, so this thinking goes, and we must do everything in our power to continue down this path of development.

Here, Communist China has assembled a most impressive cadre of American elites to support its way of thinking. This is its real achievement.

Our Problem Today:
The Moral Corruption
of American Elites

To be clear, the very real crisis we find ourselves in today with Communist China would not be possible were it not for the moral corruption of American elites in our universities, in business and finance, and in our government. Some of this corruption comes from within; some is cultivated by the Communist Chinese. Understanding this is central.

America is a nation born of the simple proposition that all men are created equal. To defend this principle, the American Revolution overthrew British rule, a Constitution was written and ratified, and for more than 250 years, we have engaged in an experiment in self-government that has brought more freedom and prosperity to more people than at any other time in human history.

The crisis in American politics is the rejection of these founding principles and the embrace of the modern progressive movement that began at the end of the 19th century, took root in the 20th century, and has near full control of the American political system today. It rejects the notion of human equality, natural right, and the notion that human beings can govern themselves.

China would prefer a deeply internally divided United States that is discredited in its use of diplomacy and military force abroad.

Although most Americans still believe in America's principles of human liberty, self-government, and natural law (however little they are taught in American schools), it is the overarching view in American universities and among American elites, that these founding principles are mere remnants of a bygone age. They believe America is better off now that it is run by experts in politics, social science, medicine, agriculture, economics, and the like; that the modern administrative state's growth and the embrace of progressive ideology has liberated the country by applying rational intelligence to discern the great questions of our age. Amazingly, the country still works despite so many influential people believing this view.

Since the end of World War II, America has assumed the role as both global economic leader and defender of a global world order in defense of human freedom. Alongside our economic success, the U.S. dollar has become the world's most stable currency, Wall Street its most desirable capital market, and American universities the hub of innovation, technological development, and higher education. The reason for this (despite the growth of the administrative state) is the strength of our constitutional order, the relative stability of our political system, and our respect for the rule of law. This system is what is under attack by Communist China.

The Chinese do not see the American experiment in free government, or democracy in general, as something to which all men should aspire. They are in the process of perfecting a form of communism to their liking. And, as far as they are concerned, American judgments about this are all rather beside the point.

The Chinese see America and the West as the source of wealth and technological advancement, nothing more and nothing less. When they study what we do or send their children to our universities, they have a very specific purpose, which is to learn how they, too, can become wealthy and technologically advanced. What America gets out of this transaction is not at all clear.

American universities, with a total population of almost twenty million students, have today almost 370,000 Chinese nationals attending their undergraduate and graduate programs. Like many students from other nations, the vast majority of these Chinese students pay full out-of-state tuition fees which, for the universities, account for enormous amounts of revenue. This is often given as the rationale for why foreign students, especially those from the P.R.C., are allowed in such high numbers. Although this practice often pushes out less affluent American students, it allows the universities to boast that they are keeping down tuition costs. Even so, a substantial number of students, especially graduate students from the P.R.C., receive full scholarships to American universities which, in the interest of getting the top students, disregard the country of origin. It should come as no surprise that President Xi Jinping's own daughter, Xi Mingze, graduated from Harvard University.

Overwhelmingly, these Chinese students are not coming to study political science, history, or American literature. They are here to become engineers, physicists, computer scientists, and the like. Although we hope they might get exposed to the principles of human freedom (the true underlying reason for the success of the United States) they are instead, in those few humanities courses they are required to take, just as likely to be lectured to by a generation of American professors (who are themselves schooled in postmodernism and progressive ideology) on some variant of the well-worn theme that America is immoral, racist, exploitative, and imperialistic. Not only are we facilitating the transfer of our technological know-how to these Chinese students, we are also schooling them in ever-advanced forms of anti-Americanism.

Even more troubling is that each of these students knows he or she is subject to the P.R.C.'s National Intelligence Law of 2017, specifically Article 7, which requires that "any citizen shall support, assist, and cooperate with the state intelligence work." It is rather remarkable that the Chinese Communist Party decided to codify such a law knowing that someone in the United States might wonder what implications it might have for the 370,000 Chinese students attending American universities, and the hundreds of thousands that would be doing business in the U.S. in the future. It is quite literally the law that all Chinese students in American universities are agents, or potential agents, of the Chinese Communist Party and the intelligence apparatus of the P.R.C.

The hard reality is that no Chinese student is beyond the reach of Chinese intelligence. Indeed, they must check in on a regular basis with the Chinese consulate, where intelligence gathering takes place. Even the most well-intentioned students are pressured by the Ministry of State Security to obtain proprietary information produced in research universities, or personal information about their professors and fellow students. These Chinese students are also required to make regular contact with Communist Party members operating in the United States for the sole purpose of maintaining discipline and further intelligence gathering. Considering the sophistication of Chinese intelligence, and the access it has to students' families back home in China, extending China's police state to American campuses is not that great a stretch.

Normally, trying to prevent such espionage against the United States is the task of the FBI and its Counterintelligence Division. But, given the sheer number of Chinese students that are here, this task is near impossible. In addition, as much as we would like to think these students are coming to the United States to learn about freedom, liberty, and justice, we need to recognize that the majority are, in fact, the children of the Chinese Communist Party's ruling elite who themselves will be the next generation to occupy the reins of power in China's totalitarian superstructure. There is a real danger for the United States in credentialing this many

Chinese students who will have access to influential parts of American commerce and society for decades to come. For a Chinese person to say they graduated from an American university is to be accepted, almost without reservation, by large parts of American society.

In a perfect world, those innocent and deserving Chinese college students could be

---

China wants to manage America's decline as a world power.

---

separated from those who believe in, and could be working for, the Chinese Communist Party. This is not practical. The potential for harm to the United States, and the real theft of intellectual property that occurs, outweighs any benefit that American colleges enjoy by way of increased tuition revenues. Reevaluating whether Chinese students ought to attend American universities at all is long overdue, especially after the impact of the Wuhan virus on American society. Part of this reevaluation has to focus on the role the Confucius Institutes play on American campuses.

CONFUCIUS INSTITUTES

A key component of Chinese strategy is the mainstreaming of Chinese cultural norms into American society, especially among young Americans. Chinese intelligence has made substantial investments in American universities by setting up more than one hundred Confucius Institutes that are designed to spread knowledge of the Mandarin language, Confucius philosophy, and Chinese culture. In reality, they are vehicles almost wholly operated by the Chinese Communist Party to recruit sympathetic Americans, shape American opinion about the Chinese government, and exert pressure on the universities to suppress any lectures, student activism, or scholars who might be critical of the Chinese

Communist Party or the P.R.C. in general.

These institutes complement the Chinese Students and Scholars Associations on American campuses. Both are used to extend the influence of the CCP beyond the 370,000 Chinese students attending these universities. Their ability to facilitate exchanges between the P.R.C. and American academic institutions – especially research universities – is critical to the operation of this intelligence network. They provide cover by offering lucrative grants to compliant American scholars whose scientific research they might want to access or the ability to sponsor P.R.C.-based students and scholars who will attend conferences where they can form professional relationships with their American counterparts.

The technological and scientific piece of this aside, there is also much to be gained by influencing the purely academic side as well. After all, the foreign policy and national security infrastructure of Washington, D.C., is shaped by the schools of international relations, themselves sympathetic to China and the globalist world view. It is not out of charity that the P.R.C. makes strategic donations to key departments in universities around the country. Bloomberg estimates direct P.R.C. grant-making at more than $1 billion, which does not even account for Chinese corporations looking to shape the debate on campus by making targeted "donations" to those many think tanks in Washington, D.C. that are filled with retired senior U.S. military officers and diplomats who form a pro-globalist chorus all of their own. Expenditures to project what China calls its use of "soft power" range as high as $10 billion a year, by some accounts.

Chinese students and the Confucius Institutes are one aspect of the problem. Another is the Thousand Talents Plan.

THE THOUSAND TALENTS PLAN

Established in 2008 by the Central Committee of the Chinese Communist Party, the

Thousand Talents Plan (TTP) has been described by the U.S. Department of Justice as a "Chinese-government talent recruitment program." Its goal is, quite literally, to recruit and cultivate the most talented people, most of whom are Chinese, to build the research, scientific, and entrepreneurial capacity of the People's Republic of China. This includes experts in the public and private sectors, in laboratories and research institutions, and in those fields deemed essential for the advancement of the Chinese Communist Party.

With a name like Thousand Talents Plan, it seemed to many like a glorified (if awkward) variation on the MacArthur Fellows Program that rewards talented scholars, artists, social scientists, writers and the like with grants to pursue their creative endeavors. Unlike the MacArthur Fellows Program, the TTP is designed to achieve global domination for the Chinese Communist Party by aggrandizing to the CCP the most talented thinkers in a variety of fields. They will be loyal to the Party either because they are being paid large sums of money, are provided with research support and the use of scientific labs and the like, or even better, are ideologically aligned with the views and ambitions of the CCP. Two of the 7,000 members of the TTP illustrate the problem of what the FBI has described as a "non-traditional espionage program."

Professor Charles Lieber

In January 2020, as the Wuhan virus was spreading throughout the United States and the rest of the world, Dr. Charles Lieber was arrested and charged with making a materially false, fictious, and fraudulent statement. Dr. Lieber was chair of the Department of Chemistry and Chemical Biology at Harvard University. Lieber was also a member of China's Thousand Talents Plan, although he consistently denied, or was unclear about, whether he was actually part of the program.

Lieber began a five-year contract from November 2011 through November 2016 with the Wuhan University of Technology (WUT)

It has become ever clearer that Communist China knew of the Wuhan virus's severity and facilitated its spread around the world.

to be a "strategic scientist." In April 2012, he was notified he would also be awarded a three-year contract to be part of its Thousand Talents Program. According to an official statement by the U.S. Department of Justice in January 2020: "Under the terms of Lieber's three-year Thousand Talents contract, WUT paid Lieber $50,000 per month, living expenses of up to 1,000,000 Chinese Yuan (approximately $158,000 at the time) and awarded him more than $1.5 million to establish a research lab at WUT."

At WUT, Lieber's role was to recruit and cultivate top PhD students to produce high-level scientific research. He was also required to work nine months out of the year in this effort. Quite a workload for someone who had a full-time job at Harvard University.

The real problem was that Lieber had been given more than $15 million in grants from both the National Institutes of Health and the U.S. Department of Defense to do specialized research in nanoscience and nanotechnology. The terms of his grant agreements with these two U.S. government agencies required disclosure of potential conflicts of interest with foreign governments, such as Lieber's contract with the WUT. It was here that Lieber failed to come clean about the extent of his work in Wuhan.

Dr. Lieber's value to the P.R.C. was obvious. He was about as accomplished and credentialed a scientist as could be imagined; the prestige of having someone like him was immense. It sent a very important signal to the American academic and scientific communities about the kind of benefits one could enjoy from good relations with the P.R.C.

and its Thousand Talents Plan. Even more significant, the WUT would likely enjoy the benefits of the research Lieber was doing in his work for the $15 million NIH and DOD grants since those began in 2009 and ran through 2018. It was quite possible that for his part, Lieber saw this merely as one more scientific project and the opportunity to expand his research and influence with the creation of a new laboratory. Regardless, it was clear that neither U.S. national interests, nor those of Harvard University, were going to be well served by having a star scientist like Lieber advancing the scientific knowledge base of Communist China.

Also, as an example of China's use of America's academic institutions as vehicles for the theft of intellectual property and scientific information, it should be noted that the U.S. Department of Justice, in announcing Lieber's indictment, also indicted Yangquing Ye and Zaosong Zheng in unrelated cases. Ye lied in her visa application about being a member of the Chinese Communist

Party and a lieutenant in the People's Liberation Army. Posing as a student at Boston University's Department of Physics, Chemistry, and Biomedical Engineering, she sent sensitive U.S. documents and information to China. Zheng was arrested for trying to smuggle back to China twenty-one vials containing the results of cancer-cell research he had done at Beth Israel Deaconess Medical Center in Boston. That such cases have become ever more routine should be of great concern to most Americans.

Yu Ben Ming

The second example of the potentially corrupting influence of the Thousand Talents Plan is Yu Ben Ming, the Chief Investment Officer (CIO) of the California Public Employee Retirement System (CALPERS). Born in Communist China and now a naturalized American citizen, Yu oversees $400 billion in assets and manages 400 employees at the country's largest public pension fund. Yu is an accomplished investment professional who held a senior position at Barclays before joining CALPERS in 2008. As part of the TTP, he left for a three-year stint in China from 2015–2018, where he managed $3 trillion in currency reserves for China's State Administration of Foreign Exchange. Yu rejoined CALPERS in 2018 as CIO.

Like many American investment professionals, Yu does not see a conflict investing in both the U.S. economy and that of the P.R.C. Part of the retirement portfolio he manages for CALPERS is invested in Chinese companies, most of whom are tied to the Chinese Communist Party and the People's Liberation Army. To give him the benefit of the doubt, he sees such investments as merely diversifying the portfolios of his retirees. As the thinking goes, individual stocks and indices are on the rise in the so-called emerging markets, and American investors don't want to be left out of the profits that can be made.

But the reality of the situation is that placing billions of dollars of state employee retirement funds in Chinese companies, most of which are state-owned enterprises, is investing in the long-term success of Communist China and its global ambition to displace the United States as an economic and political leader. It strengthens the Communist Party's hold on Chinese society, continues its repression of internal dissent, and facilitates its military and technological build up. Today, every major business entity in China has Communist Party cells within it in order to ensure that the Party's interests are achieved.

Yu, of course, knows all this. He is not some junior investment analyst. He is, quite literally, one of the most influential investment managers in the world. For this reason, he has attracted some attention, especially from Jim Banks, congressman from Indiana, who called on California governor Gavin Newsom to look into Yu's work for CALPERS, given the new scrutiny of where state and federal retirement funds are being invested. Of special import was an interview Yu gave to the Chinese newspaper *Society*

People when he joined the Thousand Talents Plan in 2015. There, Yu was quoted as follows: "In a person's life, if there is an opportunity to serve the motherland, this kind of responsibility and honor cannot be matched by anything."

Certainly, this does not make Yu an agent of the P.R.C. There are plenty of investment managers more than willing to invest in Communist Chinese companies. It is, therefore, not surprising that Stephen Schwarzman, CEO of the private equity firm Blackstone (which is also heavily invested in China) came to Yu's defense after he received criticism for his investment policies. But this also does not absolve Yu, and those like him, that either fail to see Communist China for the dictatorship that it is, or, knowing this, decide to continue investing in it anyway.

The scope of this problem has been well-explained by former Reagan administration official Roger W. Robinson, who served as the senior director of international economic affairs on the National Security Council.

Robinson has been focused for some time on not only the short-term benefits to Chinese corporations of these U.S. investments, but their long-term implications for U.S. statecraft and national security policy.

Imagine a day when trillions of dollars held in American retirement funds are tied up in Chinese equities, Chinese sovereign debt, the debt of China's state-owned enterprises, or market indices that contain such investments. In the event of any confronta-

---

Imagine a day when trillions of dollars held in American retirement funds are tied up in Chinese equities.

---

tion between the U.S. and the P.R.C., enormous pressure will be put on an American president not to hold China to account; for instance, lest it have financial implications for a substantial number of American retirees. America's long-term strategic concerns will become secondary to the short-term financial success of individual investors. The prospect of this is not at all far-fetched.

The People's Republic of China was, by late 2019, reportedly considering approaching Wall Street with an estimated one to three trillion dollars in new sovereign bond offerings, as well as bond offerings of their state-owned enterprises, over a three-year period. For its part, the P.R.C. needs the capital. No doubt, Wall Street investment houses certainly will be interested in the commissions they will receive from such huge offerings. Understanding the political implications of such transactions is limited to those few national security professionals who see danger in further entangling the U.S. economy with China's.

On the other side, of course, are those Wall Street investors who are deeply invested in both Communist China, and globalism more broadly. Larry Fink, chairman of Black-

Rock, Steven Schwarzman, chairman of Blackstone, and Henry Paulson, former secretary of the Treasury and now head of the Paulson Institute, form a phalanx around Communist China, protecting it as best they can from U.S. policymakers trying to contain China's economic malfeasance. The investments of all three dwarf those of Yu Ben Ming and CALPERS. Given the intimate relationship of the world of finance with the world of politics, it is quite remarkable that President Trump has been so aggressive in checking China's theft of intellectual property and establishing a more reciprocal relationship with the P.R.C.

It is not that surprising that Americans who have become billionaires from their business dealings with Communist China seek a continuation of friendly relations. What is surprising is that these global asset managers have any standing with U.S. policymakers, given what has to be such a glaring conflict of interest. One has to be concerned about having Americans deeply invested in

Communist China. So, too, must we be concerned about our billionaire class and its similar entanglements with Communist China.

BlackRock alone has $7.4 trillion of assets under management. How much of that is invested in the P.R.C. and in the P.R.C.'s economic designs? Additionally, what could it portend that Fink and BlackRock were given management of $4 trillion from the Federal Reserve to help deal with the economic crisis caused by the Wuhan virus? The concentration of money and power, beyond the financial understanding of both everyday citizens and their elected representatives in Congress, should be of great concern.

There are a thousand more examples, high and low, of Chinese agents of influence in the U.S. Lieber and Yu are the tip of the iceberg. If there is any silver lining in the awful consequences of the Wuhan virus and the pandemic of 2020, it is the complete rethinking of America's relations with Communist China.

President Trump stated in early February 2020 that he was a wartime president – the war being with an invisible virus. As time has gone on and it has become ever clearer that Communist China knew of the Wuhan virus's severity and facilitated its spread around the world – most especially to the United States – the President's tone has changed markedly. He is still a wartime president, but the invisible enemy now rather clearly appears to be the Chinese Communist Party. To put it mildly, the U.S. has entered a new phase in its relations with the People's Republic of China.

One indicator is a letter sent on May 11, 2020, from Larry Kudlow, national economic advisor, and Robert O'Brien, national security advisor, to Eugene Scalia, secretary of labor. In the letter, they recommend against investing the funds of federal employees that are held in the Federal Retirement Thrift Investment Board's Thrift Savings Plan in Chinese companies. Their reasons are numerous, from potential sanctions stemming from China's culpability over COVID-19, to the lack of transparency caused by China's law prohibiting outside audits of its companies, and its unwillingness to comply with the requirements of the Securities and Exchange Commission and the Public Company Accounting Oversight Board. Additional concerns focus on Chinese companies' human rights abuses and their ties to the People's Liberation Army.

Until this letter by Kudlow and O'Brien, which was certainly written at the direction of President Trump, China had largely avoided such scrutiny. Such was the desire of America's financial elites to continue their economic relations with the P.R.C. This is all now being reconsidered. The ramifications for Wall Street and for the American economy overall, devastated by the lockdown and the pandemic, are still being studied. What is clear is that every facet of the U.S.-P.R.C. relationship is now under review.

Left mostly undiscussed here are the efforts by the P.R.C. to corrupt high-ranking U.S. government officials. As Joe Biden's presidential campaign heats up this fall, Americans will learn more about how the investment firm run by his son, Hunter, received $1.5 billion from the Bank of China. Also undiscussed here are China's transparent efforts at intimidating Hollywood and popular entertainment. Witness the treatment the NBA received in China after Daryl Morey, general manager of the Houston Rockets, tweeted his support for the pro-democracy protestors in Hong Kong. Even during the pandemic, this harassment continues.

What is clear is that more than a few Americans believe that the spread of the Wuhan virus was a deliberate attack upon the United States and that Communist China ought to pay for what it has done.

To be sure, no one is interested in war with Communist China. That would be a bloody and awful affair that would dramatically alter Americans' way of life even more than this pandemic has done. But it appears a war has begun all the same. What will be required is moral clarity about friends and enemies both inside and outside the United States as it relates to Communist China. It will require hard choices about who attends American universities, who should be allowed

The inevitable rise of China has turned into the inevitable conquest of the world by the P.R.C.

in the country, and what steps should be taken to ensure the peace and prosperity of the American people.

All of these things are well within the capacity of the American people and their representatives to understand and to address. These steps must be taken now before it is too late.

First American edition published in 2020 by Encounter Books,
an activity of Encounter for Culture and Education, Inc.,
a nonprofit, tax exempt corporation.
Encounter Books website address: www.encounterbooks.com

Manufactured in the United States and printed on
acid-free paper. The paper used in this publication meets
the minimum requirements of ANSI / NISO Z39.48–1992
(R 1997) (*Permanence of Paper*).

FIRST AMERICAN EDITION

LIBRARY OF CONGRESS CATALOGING-IN-PUBLICATION DATA
IS AVAILABLE